DEDICATION

This book is dedicated to my mother, father, sister, nephews, two grandmothers that are in heaven, Irene Johnson, Ruth B Lee, my Godmother Gertrude Woodard, my Grandfather Theodore Johnson, to everyone that was riding with me before I got shot and lost my ability to walk, to those that are no longer riding with me after I got shot, to those that love me, and those that hate me or hate on me this book is dedicated to you too.

TABLE OF CONTENTS

MY PRAYER

Thank you, Lord, for keeping me alive and still strong as I
ask for forgiveness for all of the things that I've done wrong.
I'm thanking you right now for sparing my life to see
another day. I thank you for last night, allowing me to sleep
tight, and keeping the death angel away.

I try my best to pray, to stay in contact, so that I can
interact, with you to find out what you want me to
do today.
I try to stay focused and keep my head above the clouds.
Trying to live my life right so that I'll make you proud.

For me and my family, I want everyone around me to see
that I am a child of you.
So the people will know that you are true.

What can I do when I have obstacles in my path?
What can I do when it seems hard for me to get on the right
track and take the right path?

I try my best to do good deeds and to make the devil go
away from me, but the temptations are great, much like my
faith, that you will help me to see that the path that I'm on
just might be wrong.

Still, I'm proud to be here. This is my prayer: I'm asking
O'Lord for you to bless me and keep me near to thee.
AMEN
02052001

FRED LEE (12 YEARS OLD)

My name is Fred Lee
I am Blac, I am the one and only Mac
I lose women but I get more bacc
Cuz my name is Fred Lee and I am Blac

PAST

Never take anything for granted.
One moment it is there and the next moment,
you may not have it.
Be grateful to be on this planet.
Life is too short to go around being mad at
The slightest little thing that you may not be able to change.
Cherish every single moment and take pride in the joy
that it brings.
Never make the same mistakes twice. Always do your best so
that you can enjoy your life!

MY MIND (PART ONE)

Come with me at this time as I take you into my mind
And try to make you realize what really goes down.

I stay on the South
I have relatives on the North
I'm really a gangbanger, so playa what are you talking about?

I've never been to jail.
I did help my cousin make bail.
Man, it is hard living in this world as a black male.

However, it really doesn't bother me. I graduated from Evan
E.
Hopefully, a couple of years from now everybody will
know Fred Lee.

My life has not been right. That's why I pray every night On
May 2, 1996, I got hit on my homeboy's bike.
By a white sidekick jeep -- sometimes at night I can't sleep --
That same day a 10-year-old boy got hit and died, and that
could've been me.

I thank the Lord I'm here. I'm glad that I'm no queer.
And, you know what, in my heart, I have no fear.

I lost three essential ladies that played a significant role in
my life.
One died on my 18th birthday and the other on a November
night.
Right before Thanksgiving Day in 1998, he took her life
away.
My other grandmother died in 1994 on a hot August day.
When it was time to go to her house, I hated to stay.

Now the only lady left is my mother.

If the Lord were to take her away, that would hurt because I
love her.

I loved those three ladies, too.
One Godmother and two Grandmothers -- Tell me how you
would react if you were in my shoes.
I try to keep my cool.
That is why I do the things that I do.
Like smoke weed to get high and hang with my homies
acting a fool.

Sometimes I chill by myself with a mean mug on my face,
But that doesn't mean I'm not happy. It's just because I've
journeyed a long way.
I really don't have a lot of time to finish this rhyme; These
are just a few things that have happened in my lifetime. So
join me next time when I'll have some more to say about
the mind of a brother who just likes to parlay

To be continued....
01101999

MISSING YOU

On November 23, just before the sun was about to set.
The Lord told my grandmother to come on and get some rest.
He took you away from this small but loving family.
You were the goddess on this earth,
Our best friend, Ruth B. Lee.
You were loving and caring, the one that we adore.
But now you are gone, and we are missing you more and more.
8320 was where you laid your head and went to sleep. But
now you walk the streets paved with gold, Worshipping
Jesus every day of the week.
Tears are not enough to express your loss!
But you ran a good race and also paid the cost.
Missing you, missing you, every day that goes by.
But now you are an angel, and with your wings you can fly.
Your physical appearance is no longer something that we can
see, but your spirit will forever be with us, Ruth B. Lee.
It seems like just yesterday when we saw your loving face.
But now you are upstairs with the good Lord and his grace.
Life will not be the same without you in the pictures. I
know personally that everybody and their mother will miss
you.
The star in the sky, the moon at night,
The most beautiful person to ever walk this earth,
The one everybody likes.
Your friends will miss you, but no one as much as me.

We all love you "Grandma," the shining star, Ruth B. Lee
11241998

I WANT TO GET OUT

The walls are caving in; I can almost touch the ceiling. The
room is getting smaller; it's getting harder for me to breath
in it. They don't care about me! They act like they can't
hear my cries for help. Why are they laughing at me? Is it
because I'm struggling to help myself?

I'm trying to reach the door before the door closes.
The faster I think that I'm moving, in reality, \
I'm moving slow.
I take one step forward, but two steps backward. How
can I go anywhere when my legs appear to be
shackled?

The window is open, so maybe I'll try that.
Oh, man, I'm hallucinating! There's no window there. Now
I'm trying to get out through the air vent, but the opening is
too small.
I can barely get one hand through, so I know my body will
not fit at all.

Oh well, guess, I'm stuck.
I have to make the best of this bad luck.
What's this? That window is open. That's not good
because I'm on the 14th floor.
There are no ledges for me to cling to so if I jump my life
would be no more.

What do I do? Do I try to make that leap?
I don't have to do that because an angel opened the door for
me.
Now I'm free.
20070120

GOD IS JUST A PRAYER AWAY

Just a closer walk with thee; that's all that I need. Although I'm not a preacher, I try to spread the word to some people that I meet.

Some people listen, but some don't

They want to talk about me just like they talked about my Lord's son.

But that's ok because I'm still going to spread the word anyway

There's an old saying, "God is just a pray away." I just told that to someone, and they asked me, "Why are you preaching to me today?" "Do you think I need prayer?"

I told her, "We all need to pray so that we can get there to that place that has golden roads."

I also let her know that she doesn't need to put her trust in man because men will fail you

She said, "Guess what, that means you."

I told her, "Yes it does and the rest of all the humans too." The only one worthy of our trust is God

I know that personally because he's been there for me through it all.

He picked me up and dusted me off and told me to spread the good news to the next one I come about.

Don't get it twisted I'm far from perfect matter of fact I may be worse than you

But the big picture is the fact that I believe in God, I pray to him, and I'm not ashamed to ask him to help me to get through.

I'll pray for you too, but you can pray for yourself better than I can because I'm not physic, and you can tell God what you need better than I can.

Prayer is the key to the kingdom and faith will unlock the door

So the question that I would like to leave to everyone is
how much faith do you hold?
20031001

ALL ABOUT YOU

So beautiful, so sexy, the love of my life, the only woman
for me.
You brighten the room whenever you enter.
There is none other that can compare to thee.
Soft as tissue, more amazing than amazing, Fine
as gold, precious as a newborn baby.

You can call me selfish because I don't want to share you;
How many guys do you know want to share their one and
only lady with another dude?
I want to spend the rest of my life with you;
I hope that you're sincere when you tell me the same thing,
too.

I'm mesmerized by your beauty, fascinated by how you do
me.
I long for you and lust for you. I love you so much; I'd give
my life for you.
If I had one lung and you needed it to live,
I'd give it to you because I love you, woman.

I hate that it took me this long to get smart;
I'm so thankful you didn't leave me so that I could start
To learn to love someone. I'm glad that it's you. You
don't know how happy I am that you didn't leave me
when I told you to.

Since I'm not trying to push you away, I'm going to do
everything to make you stay;
I promise to be the best man as long as you let me occupy
your space.

My world is your world, it's all about you, baby.

Whatever it is that you want, don't hesitate to ask me, lady.

I'll do whatever I need to do to prove my loyalty to you;
My only request is that one day, maybe, you'll love me like
you used to.
1200721

AWAY

I wish to get away and go to a place unknown to man for
me to stay.
I want to move out of the south side, from my hood, known
as R E, maybe I'd go stay in Brazil or Turkey.
I would consider going to another state such as New York
or the Hawaiian plates.

I wish to get away so that I can explore new places and see
new faces.
When I turn 18, I'll go live on my own. Then I won't have
my mother worrying about what time I'm coming home.
I'm not saying that I'll never come back, but since I Am
Blac, I want to see if I'm really a Mac.

When I go away I'll get to explore new environments and
finally get the chance to see how the other side of the world
lives.
I get high as a kite to soothe my mind, but I know that that
will stop in just a matter of time.
Away is where I wish to be, whether it is with other people
or just me, this 17-year-old chasing green.

I plan to take long vacations and trips to new countries,
who knows maybe I'll end up chilling in Germany.
I'll go nowhere if the Lord is not on my side;
If I don't have him with me, then I don't want to ride.
Away, I'll say again is where I want to go, but I don't know
where, neither do you, only God knows.
06231998

FOR MY SISTER'S WEDDING

I wish you happiness, joy, and nothing, but the best. I wish
you peacefulness, calmness, and for your marriage to be a
success.
There will be good days and bad days, but don't let that led
you astray.
There are going to be smooth seas and rough tides but
remember your vows you shared on today.

I'm glad that you found someone who is down and someone
that loves you for you.
I'm happy that he has this swagger about him that seems so
humble and true.
We are all searching for true love and congratulations your
search is over.
When I look into both of your eyes, I see that you're both
high off love and not sober.

Together forever, that is my prayer for both of you. I
truly believe in my heart of hearts that the love that you
two share is what will carry you through.
Take care of him, and he will take good care of you. With
that in mind, you should be together until time decides to
no longer move.
May you grow old together and let nothing or no one
separate you two.

Stay prayerful and thankful to God, and that should make
your cloudy days turn blue.
I'm so happy for the both of you, and I think that everyone
else here is, too.
So I'll leave by saying, "Happy trails to the both of you."
08200703

JAMMED UP

As I sit back and gaze out the window, my mind goes back
to the time when I was little.
No worries, no stress, just curiousness was my asset. But
that was back then when I was about 10.
Now I'm 21, knocking on 22, fresh out on bail, from my third
time going to jail, charged with just 5 oz. of some good. What
a fool I was to be riding with some bud. Now my future lies
in the hands of some judge.
Hopefully because I'm a first-time offender, the judge will
be lenient and give me a light sentence.
Probation I don't want, but if I have to, I'll jump on it.
Hopefully, I can do weekend time, so I can still be blowing.
One thing's for sure, whatever the outcome may be, the
person I was riding with can no longer ride with me.
Jammed up by the same two cops that I said, "what's up,"
Don't worry, I'll never speak to another officer again.
I already did not like them but at least I showed respect.
Now I have no love for them because he pulled me over
talking about this is a traffic check.
No warrants, no problems, no reason did I give, yet and still
they took advantage of their authority and felt the right to
send
Me to jail for the third time in four years for three different
reasons,
So I've come to the conclusion, while I'm still breathing, to
stay as far away as I can from the police people.
041103

INSIDE

Stuck inside this room like air trapped in a balloon.
No contact with the outside world either verbally or with a view.
Imagine not seeing a tree or feeling the wind blow or hearing
the sound of people talking or even the horns from the vehicle's
blow.
Stuck in this room and I'm aware of what's happening, but I
feel so helpless because I can't seem to tell what's
happening.
What can I do to get out of this room? I do what the doctors
tell me, but nothing seems to be helping me to get through.
Or over that hump, laying in a bed in a slump, back aching
with pain; pain so unbearable that I can't even scream all I
can do is grunt.
It seems like no one cares when I'm in this room
I press the little button to call for help, but it seems like it
takes the help forever just to come through.

Sometimes I wonder, "Do the nurses even care?" Then I get a
good nurse's assistant and they let me know that they are there.
Not just for a check, but for the well-being of the patient.
While the head nurse that makes more money than the
assistant will barely take time to listen.
They come and introduce themselves to me then I will not
see them for a while, because they are sitting on their rump,
drinking coffee with a big Kool-Aid smile. The best time in
the room is when I get a visitor. I cherish every person that
comes by to see me because they seem to make it be a little
bit easier.
The company of people, the value of life, all the things I
took for granted, I cherish with all my might.
Stuck in a room with visions of getting outside, I do believe
that as long as I keep my faith, the good Lord will take me
away from this inside. 20050507

TRYING TO QUIT

Trying to quit smoking, I'm not joking, just hoping to keep
coping, once the smoke stops blowing.
Praying I don't go off because my nerves are bad;
My attitude is cool; I just hope not to get mad;
At the slightest little thing hoping not to eat that much to
take away the pain.
I work at a call-center, so much stress on my brain;
Grateful to God that I have not attempted to slice one of my
veins.
It's not because of the cigarettes or the extra-curricular
things, it's because the good Lord has kept me in the right
mind frame. I smoke a whole lot at work, so that I don't
go off on some of those jerks.
Not every customer is horrible, some are the bomb. I
promise once I stop working here I'll never work at
another one.
I wrecked my car while throwing away a cigarette. I did
something that I've never done before -- caused the accident.
Still I be puffing, matter of fact, it's worst, but I must quit
because my body just hurts.
Go to the doctor for what? I know what's wrong. One day
I'll quit because the chest pain is not fun.
20030602

Lord Help Me

Lord, help me to fix the things that I broke; Lord,
help me to realize that you are not a joke.
Lord, help me to achieve the things that seem worthwhile;
Lord, help me to live a good lifestyle.
Lord, help me to realize that you are true;
Lord, help me to do the things that you want me to do.
Lord, help me to be your servant; Lord, help me to be
a merchant.
To tell people more and more about you; Please,
Lord, help me to see things through.
AMEN
13199803

BABY I MISS U

You really don't know how much I truly miss U;
I guess, I didn't know myself until the time came and I no
longer had U.

Words cannot express how much I wish to see your face;
Every day, inside my head, I see your face and I wonder,
"Why did it have to end that way?" What more can I say?

There is nothing that I won't do to see you and get next to you.

I will never forget the day when I saw your pretty face;
That smile that you had made me glad you were my gal.
Now U are so far away, every day I sit down and pray; That
way the Lord will let us be together again one day.

In a big house with a nice car, you are my real true star.

This is no game even though it may seem lame;
But who is to blame and I'm glad U came.

Now that you're gone, sometimes it's hard for me to go on.
I will stay strong because I believe that it won't be long
Before I can see you again and make you more than just a
girlfriend.
Who knows what the future holds; I'll just sit back and let it
unfold.
19990520

LOVE

"What are you looking for," you ask as I pass;
"I'm looking for love," I reply as I'm going to class.

"Where have you looked," is what you say;
"I've looked everywhere, but now I'm parlayed."

I'm not searching for love. I believe it will come;
My only hope is the fact that it will be with the right one.

I can't let my heart go and fall in love with a hoe; I
damn sure am not going to fall in love with a brother
named Joe.

A woman is my only thing, only she can take my heart;
I just hope she's not mean and rip my heart apart.
I know I've been a playa, but I've never been a waiter.

I've never been in love, but I want to see how it feels;
My only demand is to hope that the love is real. Not
fake because my heart might not take A girl who will
try to use me like a rake.

On the winter days and summer nights, I
need the love that I know is right.
When I find it and it's real, I'll tell you how it feels.
For right now, my only true love is to smoke on some kill!
01251999

BLACK LESSON

28-29, when the year contains 365.The shortest month of the year that they set aside for the people of my kind, and that was not live.

Black History is something that should be celebrated every day.
Reason being, there are a lot of things that God allowed us to accomplish that has paved the way.
Like Lloyd P. Ray, who made the dustpan of today for all to sweep the dirt up to throw away.

The traffic light invented by Garret A. Morgan. There was a man named John Burr, that invented the lawnmower.
Ever wondered why your clothes are wrinkled no more? It's because of Sarah Boone, a black woman who invented the iron broad.

I know that we get hot in the summer and cold in the winter.
Well, remember Frederick Jones, the air conditioner inventor, and the heating furnace was invented by Alive Parker, a sister.

Is your pencil dull? It shouldn't be because the pencil sharper was created by John Love.
Still need more?
Thomas W. Stewart invented the mop, for everyone to mop Pine Sol on the floor.

And still there are more things that we offer and bring to the table.

It's a shame that we receive the shortest month of the year for celebrating.

But I'm grateful for that and happy I am, because I celebrate Black History every chance that I can.
02052003

STAYING IN THE HOSPITAL

They have to treat me better. I feel neglected;
I feel like they think that my well-being is not worth it.
They talk to me crazy and say mean things;
Why do they treat me like this? I have not done anything.
Wrong to them, they don't know me like that.
I deserve to be treated better than some kind of pack rat.
I'm not a rodent. I'm a human being;
I'm a person with needs, emotions, and feelings.

So why don't these people respect my gangsta
Some may say I'm not a G, but I promise I'm no wangsta.
I'm a soldier and I've never been in an army. The only
army I belong to is the one and only G O D and I'll stand
on the frontline.
I'm no punk so why do you try to hit me from behind? They
are really testing my patience which is not short, but far
from long.
I know that life is not fair, but the way that they treat me
here cannot continue to go on.

However, I will not trip and whine and whimper. I'm
a man, not a boy. I can handle these issues.
I'm tired of being here; I can't wait to get out;
The food is horrible, and the smell has clogged up my
nostrils.
Screaming and yelling, there is no peace and quiet
How do they expect me to rest when it sounds like there is a
riot?
What do you say I'll be leaving in a couple of days? Well,
thank you, Lord because this is not where I want to stay.
23200506

GIVE IT A TRY

Even though the clouds are gray, believe me when I say
That the sky has got to clear up someway
Because that is the way of nature just look at what God
gave us
The smiles on the kids faces, so innocent yet contagious
Seeing the little kids happy for no reason
Without a clue of what's going on
Just happy to be breathing
Through all the tough times
I found out that a smile
Can ease the pain just for a little while
Go ahead give it a try
06252006

DO ME FOR WHAT

Why do you want to do me, for what reason?
Because your man only likes to do it once a season.
Maybe that's how he likes it. You seem to
I know why you want to do me, it's because of how I do.

Maybe you want to do me because your man is a noodle. I
know that you want to have my baby elephant trunk all up
in you.
Why? I don't have anything for you.
You need to just continue doing it with your dude's strudel.

You ask me if I want to come by because I want some booty.
But I don't ask you why you sneak out while your man is
sleeping.

Do me for what? Because your man can't fucc;
And you like the way that I seem to beat it up.
You have a man at home that likes to leave you all alone.
He hit you, cheated on you, and even tattooed another
woman's name on his arm.

But you want to go bacc? I hope he has changed like he said.
I hope that he never again draws blood from your head.
You say that you're doing what's best for you and me
When I know deep down inside you're doing what's best for
you and he.

You also say that you will not call me on the phone;
Well, go on what's best for me is if you just leave me alone.

Do me for what? Don't you and your man lay up?
He comes by whenever he wants to and you're telling me
that you two don't even screw?

If he's there every day, Monday through Sunday, I know
he's not sleeping on the couch. Y'all have got to be doing
something.

If you're not doing anything, then why can't I come over?
Is it because you and he are sleeping together under the cover?

I'm not going to call you a hoe; I'm not going to call you a
bitch. I'm not going to call you a trick; I'm not going to call
you a witch. I'm not going to call you a tramp; I'm not
going to call you a slut
But the next time you do call me I am going to ask you,
"Do me for what"?
10200309

Break Up

Breaking up with you is not the easiest thing to do, but the issues that we have, I can no longer go through. The last two and half years consisted of more good than bad, but lately it has not been cool. I cannot seem to keep you from being mad.
I gave you all that I had and then some, but you keep asking me for more when I do not have none.

Lately, when I have been thinking everything is all gravy, you turn around and say something that makes me cry on the inside like a big baby.
It never fails, every time I think it's all fine and dandy, you say," Fred, you ain't doing this you ain't doing that," and I am thinking to myself, "Damn!!"
How can I give you more when I have nothing left? Truthfully, instead of going through this, I would rather be by myself.

You are a great woman, the best I ever had. If I met a million other women none of them could compare;
To you, but I think it is best that I let you go, because if I am not happy and I cannot keep you happy, then there is nothing between us anymore.

I pray and hope that the next person that comes along treats you with respect and dignity, so you do not have to sing that sad song about being all alone.
I am sorry it is over, and I am moving on now; One thing I will not do is let my guard back down.

Therefore, you have a nice life and do not expect me to come over tonight. I pray and hope that we can remain friends throughout our life.
I am out Peace.
20052005

MY MIND (PART TWO)

In My Mind Part One, the journey had just begun.
Now here is part two, the continuation of part one.
I've had some rough times in these past few years,
While I shed a few tears, I am thankful to still be here.

I saw my uncle for the first time since 1995,
But when I saw him it wasn't happy times
We were putting my Grandfather in the ground.

I lost my other uncle that was born on my birthday.
He was killed on a Monday and wasn't found 'til Friday.
He was cooler than a fan and always gave a helping hand.

My little sister had a little man making me an uncle and
His name is Ja'Mourice, he's the life of the family.
I'm also supposed to be a daddy, but her mother is
challenging.

She took the baby away and I've never seen my kid's face.
I haven't received a postcard nor phone call from her to say
that they are Okay

I've been trying to locate them, too.
Every number that I have has been discontinued. And to top
all that off, I've done nothing wrong to her for her to do
what she do.

Then there was another girl who told me she was pregnant,
too.
Dig these blues, she's married to some dude
And I just got word and it is some bad news.
The baby she had is no longer with us. She lost her life.
That's so not cool.

So still it's not peaches and cream;
Sometimes I really want to scream
Or maybe pinch myself thinking this is all a bad dream.

It's not though. It's life and life goes on, Stay
tuned holmes because this is not the last one.

To be continued...
27082002

NOW

Learn from the mistakes made in the Past so that you can move on to the Now section of your life.
Understand that some changes do not happen overnight;
Do the best that you can to live your life right. Sometimes you have to do what you don't wanna do in order to do what you really need to do.

Never allow anyone to take you away from you.

You can't take everyone with you when you are about to take that flight.

The one that catapults you into the What's Next section of your life.

MY MIND (PART THREE)

In My Mind Part One the journey had just begun; My
Mind Part Two was a continuation of part one.
My Mind Part 3 contains more about me;
I hope that you are ready to once again enter into my M-I-N-D.

So let's see, where should I start. I guess, I'll start by saying
that in the last five years I've been to jail four different
times for four different crimes, in two different states and
that is not something that makes me proud.

I have been shot at twice, luckily, they missed.
However, on June 14, 2005 I was robbed and got shot by
one of two tricks.
Shot in the neck and now I'm paralyzed from the chest
down;
I am, however, very happy to still be around.

Sometimes it is hard. Sometimes I wish I was dead; I
have to constantly remind myself that there is a brighter
day ahead.

Whenever I feel down, I just look up, and I say to myself,
"Thank you, Lord, because it could have been worse."

I do not deserve to be here; I am not all that good.
I guess, I am not all that bad because I am still here to. I do
not know why God spared my life on that hot summer
night, but I do give him all the praise and the glory
because I am still able to read, write, and type.

Life has a completely new meaning to me;
It is a shame that I had to get shot and become paralyzed to
see life differently.

The doctors say that I will never walk again. I
really do not believe that, my friends.
I believe all things are possible if you put it in God's hand.

My mind runs wild about 1,000 miles an hour;
However, as you can see, there has been a drastic change in
my life right now.

Through all of this I am still here after staring death in the
face;
So stay tuned for the next one because as long as I am here
I will forever have something to say.

To be continued....
20022006

GRACE AND MERCY

On June 14, 2005, I was shot in the back of my neck by one
of two guys.
They were trying to rob me.
I did not have anything, but about $30.00, a necklace,
watch, and ring.
I also had a work truck, could it have been a case of bad luck?
That the gentleman that shot me did not take anything, but my
$30.00 bucks?

No, it was not luck. It was the grace of God that I sit here
now telling this story to all.
I put up a fight and got shot point blank range. The doctors
said two more inches to the left, the bullet would have hit
my heart, and I could have died instantly.

However, it was not my time to go.
I had a talk that night with God and I gave him my soul.
His grace and mercy are the only reason that I'm still here.
Because those guys pushed me out of my truck, left me for
dead, and that is no lie, that is real.

God's grace kept me calm and his mercy allowed me to call
911 from my own cell phone.
I now sit in a wheelchair paralyzed from the chest down;
This is only temporary because I believe that I will be
walking again in a little while.
If you don't believe in mercy and grace of the good Lord
that is in control of this space,
Take a look at me and notice the happiness on my face.

I'm proud to still be alive and I'm glad that God was and
still is on my side;
I now have another perception about life. Please, don't be
shocked if you see some tears in my eyes.

God's mercy and grace is the only reason that I'm still here
today;
I thank him from the bottom of my heart; for He has spared
my life to live and see another day.

Matthew 26:39 Jesus says, "O' my Father, if it is possible,
let this cup pass from me nevertheless not as I will but as
you will."
This is my prayer that I say to my Father so that I can
receive enough strength to climb up this hill.
God's grace and mercy is all that I need.
It is because of his grace and mercy that I'm able to be here
to read and write more poetry.
26072005

My Appreciation to You

I appreciate you for the things that you do;
The love and support, I thank you for that too.
Blessed am I for your helping hands and countless efforts. I
know without a shadow of doubt that the Good Lord will
bless you.
Thanks for your infinite donations.
I also want to thank each and every one of you for your
patience.
Words cannot express my gratitude.
I really appreciate the fact that each time I called on you,
none of you were rude.
I truly appreciate the ideas that each of you gave.
It's because of those ideas and prayers, everything went the
right way.
I thank the Master upstairs for blessing me to work with all
of his wonderful people.
And I thank each and every one of you wonderful folks for
being there for me when I really needed you. Thanks for
not slacken off when the times got rough. I deeply
appreciate the time that you took out of your busy
schedule to help me;
I know that was tough.
Thank You, Thank You, Thank You, I cannot say it
enough. I hope that you accept this appreciation letter
designed for you, to show that I love, and I thank each and
every one of you so much.
061103

TO MY DAD: HAPPY FATHER'S DAY

Happy Father's Day to you, Mister Freddie E. Lee; The
one that keeps people cool in the summer by fixing
their A/C.
The one that warms people up in the winter by fixing their
heat.

I love you so much because of all of the things that you've
done;
I stand here **BOLDLY** and proud to be your son.
I wish I could have bought you something, but my financial
status wouldn't let me.
So I took my time to write this for you and I hope that you
accept it.

I thank my Heavenly Father for giving me the best Father in
the world.
I thank my earthly Father for helping me with life's twist
and turns.
I wish to take this time out to say Happy Father's Day to
each and every Father that's here today;
Especially the ones that put me in my place when my dad
was gone on certain days.

Some of the ladies are fathers, too, so I won't leave them
out.
I'll close by saying Happy Father's Day to every man and
woman that's down for taking care of their child.

I LOVE YOU DAD!
20062004

BABY OR ADULT

Games are for kids, but adults tend to play more;
The way that some adults act makes you believe they
should be doing the kids chores.

The Bible says: *When I became a man, I put away childish
things.*
Well, sometimes inside I think people are going insane
because their brain soaks up the games

That are ran for fun, but I'm not the playful one.
Therefore, no games have I won.

Childish as a kid, some adults act like they don't want to
grow up and live;
They'd rather spend the rest of their days being a Toys "R"
Us Kid, wanting to harass and play; I choose to bypass the
games.
It used to get to me; now it's really nothing.

I found out, over time, some people will not change;
They are 23 years old or older and still have a baby's mind
frame.

Crawling when they should be walking; babbling, when
they should be talking.

Running up your nerves like kids whining for toys;
Grown women acting like little girls, grown men acting like
little boys.

The world will continue to spin whether you decide to grow
up or buy plastic toys for yourself or your kids;

Long as you live, you are going to grow old and have to give
Up the things you used to do as a child, and realize that life is
short, so enjoy it for a while.

Grown toys are for grown people; childish toys are for
young people.

If you classify yourself as an adult, would you spend your
time buying toys for yourself that says: For Ages 1-3 years
old?
20021206

I DON'T WANT TO DIE

Cut it down the middle, take out the tobacco, fill it with
weed.
Put a lighter to it; give it life, so I can put my mind at ease.
Smoking green trees, to some it's not live.
I am thankful to be alive and I don't want to die. At
least not yet, I have plenty plans left.
Like trying to get my wealth and I bet that I'm still in good
health.

We all must go when he calls, ready or not.
Even the hardest person on the blocc has to go when he
punches the clocc.
Ready or not, he's coming and there will be no running
away.
Even if you wish to stay, the Lord is still coming
For the dead ones first, then for the ones above the dirt
And the ones that feel well, plus the ones that hurt.

I want to go to Heaven because hell is not a place I want to
dwell.
Besides, my two grandmothers went upstairs with the one
who really cares.
So to you I say, "Don't try to make me stay, or try to
provoke me to do wrong when I know the right way."

It's time to straighten up because the Lord is coming bacc.
That is no joke; these are actual facts.
08091999

DEALING WITH IT

They have got to treat me better.
I feel neglected;
I feel like they think that my well-being is not worth it.
They talk to me crazy and say mean things.
Why do they treat me like this? I have not done anything

Wrong to them. They do not know me like that;
I deserve to be treated better than some kind of pack rat.
I am not a rodent. I am a human being;
I am a person with needs, emotions, and feelings.

Why don't these people respect my "gangsta"?
Some may say I am not a G, but I promise I am no wangsta.
I am a soldier and I have never been in the army
The only army I belong to is the one and only

G O D and I will stand on the frontline;
I am no punk. Why do you try to hit me from behind?

They are really testing my patience, which is not short, but
far from long.
I know that life is not fair, but the way that they treat me
here cannot continue to go on.
I will not trip and whine or whimper.
I am a man not a boy I can handle these people.

However, it is hard. It's not easy having to deal with these
problems.
As the days go by, it is becoming easier and easier to solve
them.

I never get good news. It's always something that I don't
want to hear.

Therefore, I have come to the conclusion to just deal with
it. Have faith in GOD and believe without a doubt
That I will walk again long as I just don't give up.
20050721

WONDERING

Wondering if it's mine? Hoping
you are alive.
Wishing to hear from you just one last time.
Tell me that you are fine, and your lifestyle is live; Praying
that the two of you are keeping things in line.

Sometimes I've wondered why the grass is green, why the
sky is blue, and why people like to scream. A lot of times
I've wondered if this is the best thing, if I have the best
theme, if this is best for me.

Have you ever just wondered if there is another human
species? On the planet with rings, what type of air do they
breathe? Is it clean?

Now back to the top the first line on the page, I want to get
the record straight so people won't take it the wrong way.
It's not my fault she left with the babe.

I tried to make her stay and even wondered why – Why
did she tell me that she didn't need me anymore anyway?
That's not the way that I would want my kid raised, but
hey I'll be safe because I'm searching my own way.

I wonder if it rains because the world is dirty.
I think that's God's way of cleaning up this Earth.
I wonder who will try to hurt or help the next person up.
See me, I'm no blocker. I try to give people courage.

Mind running wild, wondering about the starving child, the
family in the cold that has to walk for miles;
Just to get turned down, because the government is full of
cowards.

I wonder a lot of things.
These are just a few.
I could go on and on, but I wish to leave some of the
wondering up to you.
20032201

LIES

I put my heart into it; put my time into it;
Put my faith into it, now I wish that I just didn't do it. Fluid
in my eyes because my time feels like it was wasted,
Now I realize and know why I do not have the patience.

For these women, who are girls, who should be playing with
my nephew's toys,
They believe that this world twist and turns around their
actions that are so foul.

I try to peep game and I seem to peep it well.
I thought the games were over with, but my nose continues to
smell
Something that is not good.
It smells like chitterlings while they are cooking;
If you have ever smelled that before, then you know where I
am going.

People think they are slick with their lies and ways, No
one do I trust in because people lie every day.
It's not hard to tell the truth, but it is easier to lie;
Then when you try to find out why they lied they try to come
up with another lie.

Habitually lie to look good; continually lie to fit in,
Constantly lie for no reason, because they are trying to make
new friends.

Lie about the people they know, lie so they can go
To hell and burn forever because they seem to like that road.
Lie to cover the truth because the truth hurts sometimes;
However, lies hurt even worse and bring tears to some eyes.

No one is perfect, so we just have to realize, pray, and hope
that the lies don't hypnotize your mind.
20020711

IF LIFE WAS A MOVIE

If life was a movie, would I press rewind, or would I let it
play instead of trying to look behind?
Or would I press fast forward to try to see the future;
Or would I press pause so that I could get used to
The life that I have that is different from the past;
The life that I don't know how long it will last.

If life was a movie, what would the script read?
Who would they use to play the life of me?
Would it be at the top of the charts, number one in the box
office? Would it be a dud because no one went out and saw
it?
Would it be rated PG13 or rated R?
Or maybe just maybe it wouldn't be rated at all.

What if life was a TV series being played once a week?
I wonder what channel it would be on, possibly ABC.
If life was a movie, where would you buy the DVD?
What stores would you buy them from, maybe Circuit City?
Or maybe online since that seems to be the biggest store. I
wonder could you buy it on eBay, and how much would
they sell it for?

If life was a movie, I'm pretty sure that it would be a whole
lot different.
However, since life is not a movie, we have to sit back and
learn to deal with it.
Life is life and there is no other way to say it.
Since life is life, I don't have to worry about what device
I'd have to use to play it.
16112005

DREAMS

Real or fake, reality or fantasy, nightmares, I hate.

Can't understand them, my friend, I can't handle them.
Sometimes I'm scared shitless because the nightmares seem
so real.

Pictures of chrome, aimed at my dome,
Waking up screaming in the middle of the night alone at
home.

I've dreamed of my life ending; Waking to a blast of light
coming from the end
Of a shotgun.
No fun.
Dreaming about someone taking my life away "holmes."

It's like staring at the GRIM REAPER with no legs to run. I
wonder if I dream like that because of the bad things that
I've done.

No sense does it make to visualize my faith;
The vision of someone killing me while I'm looking at
them dead in the face.

No sorrow in their eyes, no fear in my heart;
No pity in their expression, no reason for me to start
Wondering about death when I know we are born to die. No
reason for me to fear, because I believe I'll meet GOD in
the sky.

High is the way I stay, only to cope with the tasks of the day.
On my knees I kneel to pray, asking GOD for his mercy and
grace.

Yet and still, I feel, there must be something going on.
Maybe it's right, maybe it's wrong, but these dreams can't
go on.

I dream good thoughts too, but the nightmares are no fool. I
woke up screaming only to realize the nightmare was not
true.

Who do I tell about these horrors? Those visions of death
that I do not honor.

My solution keep my faith and pray to the Lord. Asking
him to make the nightmares go away so that I can rest in
peace, without waking up in horror, with that horrible
expression on my face.
08192002

BELIEVE

Never get your hopes up high for something that can pass
you by, never listen to a person that you know will tell you
a lie.
If it sounds too good to be true, then maybe it is. If
you want to find out if it is the truth, then give that
person a pop quiz.
They may guarantee something, but that doesn't mean that
it's real. They may be selling you a dream that's going to
send you downhill.

No one wants to be down. Everybody wants to be up. If
you are trying to bring me down, then you've just messed
up.
I let nothing stand in my way of something that I want or
need. If I don't take a stand for it, then how can I succeed?
There are only two things in life that is really guaranteed,
one is to be born and the other is to be buried.

Those are guarantees coming from the man upstairs, the
one that made me and you, and the one who really cares.
He tells no lies because he is the truth and the light of the
world; he made every last man, woman, boy, and girl.
Believe someone else if you want to be sold a dream, but I
believe in GOD if you know what that means.

He will not sell me a dream or a fake ticket to a fake land,
so if you can't believe in GOD then tell who do you think
that you can?
19992307

12-16-2006

All I asked was to be told the truth.
If the truth was told then, there would've probably been a different look
On the outcome of the situation that has my mind blazing.
"What's going on with my lady?"
I wonder if she truly enjoys treating me shady.
Then I must wonder, "why be with me?"

You don't have to continue to hit me with these low blows;
Then again, there is no such thing as a "fair fight" is what I was told. It's hard to be with you knowing that you are seeing other dudes.
To lie about it, well, that really makes it so not cool.
I LOVE YOU

I hope that one day it can go back to how it was on the first day.
I know that might not happen, so I will settle for the next best thing whatever it takes to get back that joy that you bring.
I used to make you so happy, but I guess that I'm old news.
It's one thing to enjoy the attention, but it is another thing to entertain and you going out with the dudes.
It's really another thing when I live with you.

I told you that I had some insecurities and you are not making them better.
I used to have high self-esteem, however, lately, it seems to have gone down a few levels. Every time that I come in, you're always too tired, but you go out and have good times.
You never have enough energy, but you're wide awake and ready to party with everyone except me.

I want you so much and I need you so bad, but please don't
drive me away because that is not something that I think I
can handle.
Karma is a mutha, but I'm willing to let it ride;
I truly wonder why you waited till I was paralyzed.
Why did you want me to move in with you if you were
going to mess over me?
You could have done this to me when I was walking on my
feet;
Or better yet, baby, you could have just let me be.
12200616

BUSINESS

Mind your own business and stay out of mine.
Like, you need to stop running and stop all the hiding. From
yourself and others, do what you do.
Don't try to be like me, your feet will not fit in my shoes.

I mind my own business and I leave other folks business alone.
Instead of standing outside being nosey, you should stay in your
home.
Take six months to mind your own business and take six
months to leave other folks business alone.

If you worry about others, then you will not have time for
yours.
If you worry about yours, then you will not have time to
worry about his or hers.
The world would probably be a better place if we kept to
ourselves.
By trying to mind other people's business, you might go to hell.

You won't have time to pray to the Lord;
Because you were out there wondering why someone else is
fraud.

Mind your own business and do your best;
When you get through minding yours, then lay down and
get some rest.
01051999

PAIN MEDICINE

Intense or moderate, whether you can or can't tolerate it,
If you are going through some pain some kind of way you
have to try to conquer it.
Whether it is prescribed or over-the-counter or maybe you
went out and bought it from someone on the corner;
Some way, somehow, you must try to find some medicine
so that the pain will no longer bother you.

So, what do you take when the pain really hits?
Sex, drugs, or violence to get you a fix?
How long does that work? A few hours or a couple of
minutes?
Then what?
You are right back to square one and that can't be to fun.
Now in the back of your head your thinking, "Man, that
was real dumb."

Because now the pain is back, and it is back with
vengeance;
So you go to the doctor and they decide to use you as an
experiment.
How do I know this? I'm only telling you from experience.
Hopefully, when the doctors hear this they will think about
rewriting the prescription that they supplied me. To help
me to get through this. To live is to have pain. What
medicine will you take when the pain is racking your brain?

For the best pain medicine, for the most excruciating pain,
you're going to have to get on your knees and talk to the man.
He's smarter than the doctor and stronger than any drug;
The Good Lord is my medicine when I'm bit by the pain bug.
He comes right on time to place my pain on hold

So if you haven't tried him, yet, you need to give him a try;
Otherwise the pain is going to continue to whip your
behind.
20060413

DOING WHAT I'M SUPPOSED TO BE DOING

Why am I not doing what I'm supposed to be doing? When
he chose for me to continue to live here on Earth on top of
the dirt. Living, breathing, and eating, yet, I have been
cheating.

I want to do right by all means.
I ask, "Please, Lord, will you forgive me for being a sinful
human being?
I am so sorry;

For not doing my part, when you have already done your part;"
My ending was truly my start;

To a lifestyle that I promised not to live by.
"Please, Father, do not ride by. Pass me not."
I cry inside, because my pride tends to keep me from crying
outside.
However, I do cry on the outside sometimes.

It is so hard to cope with this new lifestyle;
When I used to be able to walk, but now I have to wheel by.
It takes me a longer time to get ready and I hope that it is not
too late for my soul to be saved.

I made a promise to God and I have not done what I am
supposed to be doing.
I need to get on the ball to start doing what I'm supposed to
be doing so that my soul is not ruined;
And my body is not consumed

In fire forever;
I want to be in paradise with my Savior.
Yet, I have not been able to put down the drink and green
while trying to stay stable.

I ask, "Please, Lord, don't hold that against me.
Please forgive me."
When you call for me, please, find my name in the book of
L-I-F-E.
20051014

Faith Missionary Baptist Church

For 52 years, Faith Missionary Baptist Church has been in
existence;
For 31 of those years, I have been a member in attendance.

I love the love that is shown when I come into the
sanctuary;
The members of this congregation are so open, heartfelt,
and caring.

Always down for sharing the good word about the Lord;
That's what makes this church big even though the building
may be small.

Friends till the end, family since the beginning;
An awesome combination, a great strategy to keep on
winning.

This race that is not given to the swift or to the strong;
A race that will be won by those that continue to carry on.

This church has truly been blessed by the Almighty from up
high;
It's because of His grace that we are all still here to enjoy
the ride.

"The working church" is a name that can best describe this
place;
We are constantly on a mission to save souls here at Faith.
Trust me there is room to become a part of God's family.
He will never run out of space.

If you want to be cool, then I recommend joining this
family, too.
Having friends that love the Lord makes you wise.

You certainly will not be a fool.

Good family members and solid friends will always help
you when you are down
They will be there to pick you up and help you dust that dirt off
you to put it back on the ground.

No family is perfect; neither are the friends;
But there is a perfect God that will be there with you until
time decides to end.

So, if you don't have a family or you don't have any true
friends,

Come join hands, with the family of the Lord, so you can
enjoy, life the way that God wants you to have; that he
already had for you in his plans.
20121910

PLEASE LORD

Please, Lord, help me to make it through this storm.
I'm not going to tell you how big it is, but I will tell the
storm how big you are.

Please, Lord, help me to withstand the pain.
I know that in a little while, the sun will peep through the
clouds, and there will be no more rain.

Please, Lord, forgive me because I am a sinner. I don't
wish to be a loser; therefore, I choose to stay on your
team so that I can be a winner.

Please, Lord, have mercy on my soul.
Please, Lord, help me to stay focused on you so that I can
achieve the ultimate goal.

Please, Lord, watch over my family and friends. Watch
over my foes, too, and the ones that hate me from deep
down within.

Please, Lord, order my steps in your word.
Please Lord help me to be able to comprehend and have an
understanding of your word.
Please, Lord, give me patience and strength to make it
through these hard times.
I wish to thank you, Lord, for everything you've done,
including giving me the gift to write this rhyme.

Thank You for the storm.
Thank You for the pain.
Thank You for the sunshine.
Thank You for the rain.
Thank You for the good times.
Thank You for the bad.

Thank You, Lord, for what you did and did not allow me to
have.

Please, Lord, help me to kick my bad habits.
Please, Lord, give me the will power to say, "Fred you
don't need that."

Please, Lord, help me in every aspect that you see fit.
Lord let your will be done not mine is my final request.
AMEN
20042001

I BELIEVE

My Lord and Savior, thank you for making me.
Thank you for sparing my life even though I don't deserve
to be;
Here at this time, on this Earth with my life.

You could have let me die, but instead you allowed me one
more time.

So, I'll try my best to spread a good word.
I pray and hope that my voice will be heard.

There were a lot of things taken from me.
So, I thank you, God, every day for my limited ability.
I believe that one day I'll walk again.
I can't wait till that day comes, but for now I must be
patient and continue to live
My life to the fullest, staying focus on what I'm capable of
doing.
Being happy for the mobility that I have at this moment.

I'm dealing with it and coping with it, I'm just not
accepting it.
Please, Lord, stay with me and help me to stay positive.
God you have been there for me, so I know it will get
better.
Lord, you said that you would not give me more than I can
bear, No, not ever.

So, I'm convinced in my mind that I can make it through
this.
Please, Lord, if it is your will, please restore my leg
movement.
I'm so glad that I worship a God that's always on time.

I'm so glad that whenever I call you Lord I can always get
through on the line.

I have faith today that this is not how I will stay.
I believe without a shadow of doubt that this mountain will
be removed out of my way.
I've made it through a lot of things and it is only natural
That I feel like I'll overcome this obstacle.
09200614

WHAT'S NEXT

*Never get your hopes up high for something that
will pass you by.
Try your best to enjoy your life by doings that
you know are right.
Never be afraid to take chances, do what's necessary to be
an honest woman or man.*

*When you meet a good person, don't let them go;
That opportunity may not come bacc around anymore.
Think positive thoughts and leave the negativity alone.
If it does not feel right, then nine times outta ten
it is wrong.
God puts everyone in your life for a reason.
It's up to you to decide if they are there for a lifetime or
just for that season.
Never stop learning from the Past and the Now.
Whatever happens Next make sure that it brings you up
and not down.*

My Mind Part 4

In My Mind Part 1, the journey had just begun.
In My Mind Part 2, I decided to let the story continue. In
My Mind Part 3, I gave you more about me.
Here's My Mind Part 4, I hope that you are ready to enter this
door, so let's go.

I will begin by saying that it will never again take me this long to
put the paper to the pen.
It's been 12 years since I have allowed anyone to enter in
To this mind of mine. I tend to close it off at times, but I have to
realize that that is not the way that we were designed.

I have had a rough but smooth last few years, but at the end of the
day, I am so thankful to be able to do what I can do
In the midst of those tears, I had to sit bacc and say to myself that
there are so many more people out there that are worse off then
you.

I will be 37 in a little while and I still have never been married and
I am still without a child.
I pray on a regular basis for the Good Lord to send me a
beautiful, smart, sexy wife around my vicinity,
One that will love me and only me.
One that will be there to let me know that with her I will never
have to worry about being lonely.

I had a solid woman that truly was A1, I let her slip away from
me because of the mindset that I was on. I hope to get her bacc.
I really love that girl.
The times that I spent with her made me feel like I was on top of
the world.
If I get the chance to get her bacc, I will not do anything to lose
that woman and make us fall off tracc.

I wonder what my world would be like if I did not get shot that
night.
I was doing the best that I could to fly right.

I hate this wheelchair, but I love my life

I am launching this new book and I hope that it sells; I hope that
they enjoy the story that I am attempting to tell. I hope that it
helps someone and lets them know that they are not by
themselves.
I believe that it will because I believe that God will answer my
prayers.

My Mind Part 4 don't worry I will supply you with more. As
long as I am on this planet, I will continue to allow you to
explore
The mind of someone live;
I promise not to make you wait so long for my Mind Part 5

To be continued…
16032018

MY LESSON OF LIFE #1

More issues to fend, no one for me to lend.
There are not a lot of helping hands so I just live life the
best way I can.
Pushes and shoves coming from life, but that is just an
alarm clock telling me to wake up and act right.

The best lesson in life is life.
Life can teach you if you take the time to listen real tight.
Observe, and stay calm, get up when taken down, the ones that
don't want to make it will choose to stay face down.

True learning takes energy, passion, and a burning desire.
Therefore, we should realize that we all could make it
higher.
Think big and don't quit. There is no need to throw fits, just
shake off the negative to help you handle it.

Then think about the positive in the worst-case scenario;
These last two philosophies will definitely help you go As
far as the stars and it will make it hard, for people to bring
you down and take you out of the yard.

Of patience and of prosperity, the yard that you set for
yourself to be, a better person mentally and physically. If
we listen to life about the things that are right, then
everything will fall in place before the day turns to night.

To be continued...
02192003

TUESDAY

Life is a maze, full of twist and turns;
And lately my body has just been yearning;

For food, sex, money, not love, but a dove or swan
So that we can bounce and turn
To a destination that only the good Lord can place;
At 7:00 on Tuesday, the "laws" was all in my face.

Grace? Oh, no! Nothing but cuffs for my ass;
Then lied and said yes I may pass, Go,
not slow, fast if I dash into the grass,
Then they sent my ass to class.

In a cell in Pearland, with no water or fan,
But a nasty ass meal that taste like it came out of a can.

Monopoly maybe so, but when I passed go 225
is what I had to give to those folks.

Didn't gain, what a shame;
This time it set me bacc in the game.

Bounce back? Yes, I will -- still blowing kill.
Soon they will feel
My wrath attack;
No set back it's on Jack.
16200009

REAL

Real is non-fiction not fiction but listen.
To the real, read, and soak up the true definition.
I'm not referring to real gold are real big;
But I'm referring to real life not cartoons, you dig? Some
live life in the unreal sense
By all means necessary, don't follow this clicc.
It's a trick to get you into some unreal mix. Real love can
best be described as G-O-D.
Real hate can best be described by the devil that envies
Real Christ followers like you and me.

Life is real; some think it's not;
You only have one life to live to do what you have to do on
God's clock.
Real straight forward is how you can best describe me; I
may joke around sometimes, but I also know reality.

It's a shame that some can't tell the difference between real
and bogus;
Let alone keep their minds on real things so that they can
stay focused.
What's real to me may be unreal for you, but if it's real to a
few other people, then maybe it is true.

There's real anger, real love, real hate, real blood, real fake,
real mistakes, real people, but many more fake.
There are real religions, real faith, real conversations, and
real people to take the artificial one's place.

There's a factitious plague that's trying to take us all.
Please keep it real and help me to find a cure to get rid of
this illness going around. 20031203

BEAUTIFUL

You know you're in love when your woman is as beautiful
as a dove, soft as the clouds above.
You've been there for me and would not let me give up.
This is just a token, there are no words to describe the way
that you seem to float, and coast so gracefully like the
words that I just wrote.
Close to my heart is where I want you to stay;

I don't care what anyone else says;
You are the most extravagant person to ever occupy space.
I LOVE YOU, BABY!
THANKS FOR EVERYTHING.
2720074

SKILLS

Skills to use, skills you'll lose,
If you don't utilize the tools that God gave to you.
Two ears to listen twice as much as you talk;
One mouth to speak so that a lesson can be taught.

The skills that you have should not go to waste;
They should be used while you're here in this place.
There are skills and trades, each different from the next. No
two people are the same, so, I guess, that's why we have
contests

To see who's the best in the things that you do,
If you don't use your skills, God will take them from you.
Then what will you do when he takes them from you?
Cry like a baby and tell him that was not cool.

Fool, it's your fault you tried to keep them in a vault
And now you're mad at yourself because the combination
has been bought.

And sold to a person who took advantage of the open ocean
And waves of ideas that would have had you going
To the top, now you're stuck, out of luck with no way up.
The elevator is broke, and people laugh at you now because
you are a joke.

You wasted the gift because you were not swift;
Now you are standing on side of the road with your thump
out asking for a lift.

It didn't have to be that way, if you would have taken the
time to say, "Thank you for the skill that I have, and I'll use
it in the best way."

My skills I will use, my tools I will not lose.
So the question I leave with you is what will you do with
your skills and your tools?
10032002

INSIDE FIGHT

I've got to go, it's getting crucial. I don't think that I'll
make it;
I have to strive, to stay alive, but sometimes I can't shake it.
It's in my mind and it is not good, you see;
And I really don't want it to take over my body.

I pray every night because I know that it is right;
Because I have to talk to God like he and I are real tight.
Still there's that fight going on, between good and evil;
While evil is trying to take over, good is trying to lead me

To the right place, I know evil from good and I know
wrong from right.
If I do something that you think is wrong, maybe, I believe
it's right.

Then there's another fight between me and the system;
The one they say is out to get him.
But I'm not going to get caught up because you can always
outwit them.

Just like the Texas 7, now that was wrong.
I'm not going to judge them because I have my own life to
carry on.
But I can't do it on my own, I really need the Lord's help;
He's the good of this situation, but it's the evil trying to
make me take it to that other step.

I can't let that happen, staying strong is a must;
Because if the evil takes over, then I could go down like a
drug bust.
0120019

DO THE RIGHT THING

Do the right thing, even though it may be hard to maintain;
In this game of life, there is really no change.

So don't blame me for the bad things that you've done; It's
really all on you and how you like to have fun.

It's dumb, however, if you choose to do the wrong thing
and not use your brain for your own thinking, know what
I'm saying.

We all live in these crucial times, but it is up to you to stop
lying and tell the truth this time.

I'm not knocking you for the things that you do;
If your life is not true, I'm not the one to judge you.

Only God can help you when the times get hard;
When people act fraud, you can depend on the Lord.

Whether you are right or wrong or tell the truth or lie,
If you repent, all our sins then in time you will fly
To a better place if the Lord passes his grace; If
you believe in your heart and confess with faith.

Who's to say the difference between right and wrong? If
you believe that it is right, then is it really wrong?

I don't know, but I know that my life is not a perfect one. I
have asked for forgiveness for all of the wrong things that
I've done.

So it's up to you.
What are you going to do?
Do the right or wrong thing, tell a lie, or tell the truth?
02292000

ASK YOURSELF THIS

Is this how I want to spend the rest of my life?
Broke, disgusted, arguing, and fighting every night.
Maybe I'll get high, but what should I do?
Some grass, this powder, some rocks, or this brew?

Do I want to stay here, to collect some debt, to come out
paying even more in bills?
Am I truly happy here or am I putting on a front? Am I
doing this because it seems right when I know all the while
it's wrong?

How long is life? Can we go one day without violence? Is
the end sooner than we think because we have not paid
attention to the signs?

When the end comes what place will you call home? There
is only one or the other. There is no in-between;
I can't die for you and you can't die for me.

Do people really care, is that why they stare?
Do you feel in your heart of hearts that life is fair?
Is it better to be dead or to be alive? I guess, it depends on
how much you love your life.
If you knew that your life was going to turn out how it did
And you had the option to come out or stay in,

Which option would you have chosen; what route do you
wish to take?
Do you choose to ride with the LORD or do you choose to
go with Satan?
This is not a test, just a set of questions to ask yourself
Life might be a lot easier if we would just be truthful with
ourselves. 20062710

CHRISTMAS NOT X-MAS

The time of the year is here;
The time for all to be of good cheer.
The time that our Savior was born;
The time that we hear lots of carols being sung. The
time that we all exchange gifts;
I hope that everyone's spirit has been lifted.

There are a lot of us that don't know the true meaning of
this time; The reason that this time of the year was
designed.
I see pretty lights and lots of gifts being wrapped; I hear the
commercials playing telling you to buy this and buy that.

But still I feel that everyone doesn't know that Christ is the
reason for Christmas for real.
When you break Christmas down, it has Christ than mas;
To me, that means that Christ loves us.
When you use X-mas, where is the Christ in Christmas?

Christmas is not about presents for us because the good
Lord sent us the best gift just because he loves us so much.
There is a phrase that I came across while reading the Daily
Bread that I would like to share, hopefully, it will stay in
your head.

"Beware of keeping Christmas, but losing Christ;" So
while you are out doing Christmas shopping whether it is
day or night.
Remember that the real reason for the holiday is for the
Lord's son, Jesus Christ.
He gave us the best gift, which is life in paradise if we
accept his son and live our life right.

So I ask you this: While you are out buying all those gifts;
Have you thought about the Son of God and his word will
you uplift for his gift?
20031219

IT'S HARD

It's hard to survive, to try to stay alive.
Especially, if you are barely making it at your little 9 to 5.
So what's next, hit the block, maybe sell some rocks;
Or whatever product you can get a hold of to try to get on top.

What if you fall short while trying to double up? Do
you think it will get any easier once you are put in
cuffs?
It's hard to make it. I believe that it is even harder to give up
Because the people that depended on you, they, too, are now
out of luck.

So I try to do all that I can, being all that I am A
man, in this world that is full of scams.

Sometimes it's hard to see the scams and it's harder to get
out of them.
It's hard to know that this crackhead was once my homie
riding shotgun.
It's hard to walk one day and the next day have it all taken
away. From two young punks that didn't want a real nigga
to make it

It's hard to stay humble when dealing with a situation that
would crumple.
A weak-minded person that runs away when they see the
lighting and hear the thunder.
How much more can one person take before they start to
lose faith?
How long are we willing to wait to see if a change is going
to take place?

You have no idea on how hard it really is trying to wait on
the sky to clear, but it seems like it has been cloudy for
years.
Yet and still no matter how hard that it is, you can't give up
if you plan on moving that hill.

The harder it is now the easier it may be later. It is
probably so hard right now because God may be
testing our faith;
To see if we are going to run from the problem or stay

So no matter how hard it may be take it from me;
There is always someone there listening to you and his
name is spelled G-O-D.
12022006

DEATH

Death is not what a lot of people look at but look around
and count how many people get capped.
The world is nothing, but the walking dead and the news is
showing a lot of pictures of red.
Blood, guns, and knives everywhere that I look, then there
are killers and they seem to get hooked. On killing another
sister or maybe even a brother, they'll kill you, me, our
fathers, and our mothers.
Death is not wanted, and it surely is uninvited, but when the
time comes for me, I surly won't fight it.

It causes a lot of drama and brings a lot of tears; I want
to know if death is something that you fear. When it
takes a loved one, it gets to the heart. Death is mostly
the end, but to some it is a start.
For a person to change from bad to good or from good to
bad, I sure would hate to see my mom and dad Go on
before me because it would hurt my heart, which would not
feel good because I've loved them from the start. Death
may change the way you look at life and it just might turn
you from wrong to right.
Death is more than just a five-letter word, what is death to
you? For me, it is the world.
12011998

DEPEND

You can't depend on no one, but yourself and God; He's
the only one that I know that will help you at all. He won't
let you down in your time of need, he's the only one I can
think of that at any point in time I can go to and lean.

He won't sell you dreams like the people of today.
When they sell me dreams, I just sit back and blaze. I
try to help people, but no one seems to care;
Now that I'm struggling, to me, it just doesn't seem fair.
But neither is life, that's why I try to do right;
Every time I seem to be doing, good here comes that fight.

Back to the subject, why do these folks act ugly, and when
you ask them for something, some of the people start
cursing.
I remember when there was a time when everybody wanted
to ride with me, but now, the only ride I seem to get is the
one on my own two feet.

One day, it'll get better. Those individuals will see, and
when things get better, I'm still going to be the same me.
Just not as nice, especially to a selected few, but still that
doesn't mean that I forgot about you.
I just remembered what you've done when I was trying to
have some fun, some will say I've changed, but so did they.
I'm not the one that sold all those dreams, that made me
plot and scheme on what my next move is going to be to
counteract the jealously.
20001102

CUM WITH ME

You cum with me, I cum with you, that way it will all be
true, boo. I miss you. Hopefully, you miss me, but we can
make it up to each other sometime this week.
This is just a small poem for the one that I want, the one
that I want to have a lot of fun, that one is you, know what I
mean?

Please come and get me so that you can fulfill my dreams.
Fill my ears with your scream, making the room cloudy with
our steam. Mind going wild imaging being in between your
thighs while you're letting go of access cream Allowing you
to reach your peak, if I reach mine before you reach yours,
no need to worry, I'm not going to roll over and go to sleep.

I'll rise back to the occasion to make sure that you get yours,
baby. I'm not a lazy dude that does not know how to take
care of his lady.

I'm not the energizer bunny, but I'll have you cumming and
cumming, while I'm going and going deeper and deeper into
your magnificent ocean.
No need for you to worry, I know how to swim. I know
how to glide and move gracefully within.

No need to rush, unless, you like it like that.
My mission is to make you happy so that you'll hit me back.
That way we can do it again and again as many times as you
want. It doesn't really matter to me, just as long as you cum.

So are you ready to blast off on my rocket?
Hold on tightly and your seatbelt, make sure that you lock it.
On your mark, set, ready, go. Oh! That was the bomb!

Let's do it once more.
22200309

HAPPY VALENTINE'S DAY

Happy Valentine's Day to you;
I can't wait to see you in your birthday suit.
So beautiful and precious like the sun rising. So nice
and sincere and I have yet to figure out why
Did you choose me to be your sweet?
To occupy your time and lay with you while you sleep. One
day out of the year is not enough for you my dear.
That's why every day is Valentine's Day when I have you near.

I'm glad that I have you as more than a Valentine;
I'm also thankful for the fact that you are only mine.
My flower in a garden that is full of weeds;
My sunshine to brighten my day when it is dark indeed.
The woman that I see every night in my dream;
The person that has done so much for my self-esteem.

I've compiled a list for you to describe you and how much
you really mean.
My Marble Slab ice cream, my supreme queen;
My extreme lady, my finger that fits so perfectly in your ring.
I could go on and on, but the paper is not that long.
To describe a person like you, the words would fill up enough
pages that it would stretch from here to Hong Kong.
Happy Valentine's Day is what I wish to say.
One rose is not enough for you. You deserve the whole
bouquet.
HAPPY VALENTINE'S DAY
20041002

HAPPY TO STILL BE HERE

As I sit back and watch the funerals going down the street,
I say to myself, "That could have very well been me."

I am so happy that God has allowed me to see another day;
I guess, that's why every time I open my eyes I take the
time to pray, and I say, "Thank you, Jesus for waking me
up this morning. Thank you, Lord, for another day."

I am so happy to still be here. Even though I have no
feeling past my chest. It could have been much worse
considering I was shot in the neck.

I do have total use of my arm and hands.
So I do what I can do because I know that God has a major
plan.
He left me here for a reason and I know that in due time he
will let me know what job he has in store.
I give him all the praise because he deserves it more and
more.

I have nothing to complain about even though if I wanted to I
could
Why should I complain when I know that complaining will
not do me any good?

I do not have to still be here, but I am. Get used to it.
I am not going anywhere until the Lord tells me to do it.

There is so much to be thankful for as long as you have life.
Whenever someone asks me, "How are you doing?"
My reply is, "As long as you see me, everything is alright."

There are not enough words to express how happy I am to
still be here.

God has spared my life so I owe it all to him.

If you are not happy to be here, please, take a look at me.
If I can be happy, then why can't you be?

None of us deserves to be here. We are not all that good by
a long shot.
God has allowed us to breathe his air and borrow his time
that's on the clock.

Right now, I'm not walking, but I will not be paralyzed
forever.
Because if I don't walk here on Earth I will one day walk
around in Heaven.
20050808

STRENGTH

Please, Lord, give me the strength to endure till the end;
Please give me the knowledge to tell a foe from my friends.
Please, Lord, help me and give me the strength to know you;
Please give me the strength to do the right thing, too.

I know that I've done wrong, but in my heart, I mean right
Please give me the strength to make it through the day and
the night.

Please give me the strength to stop all my bad ways; I also
need strength to kick my bad habits so that I will not be
shorting my days.

I also need strength so that I can see things through; Plus,
the ability to know your word so that I can do what you
want me to do.

Lord, I ask for strength so that I can say good things; I
also need strength to just be happy when my pockets are
full of change.

Please, Lord, give me the strength to go on even when my
pockets are empty;
Most of all, Lord, I ask that you please stay with me.
AMEN
02072000

PEACE

Peace unto the world and peace unto you;
The world would be a better place if we let peace rule.
No wars, no fighting, no bickering, or hate;
Just love for one another; let's hold hands and pray
To the Prince of Peace and Lord of Lords, The one
who looks low from up above. Peace is love; war is
hate.
Love will keep us together;
Hate will make us separate
Peace unto the world and peace unto you; I
have peace within my heart how about you?
08302003

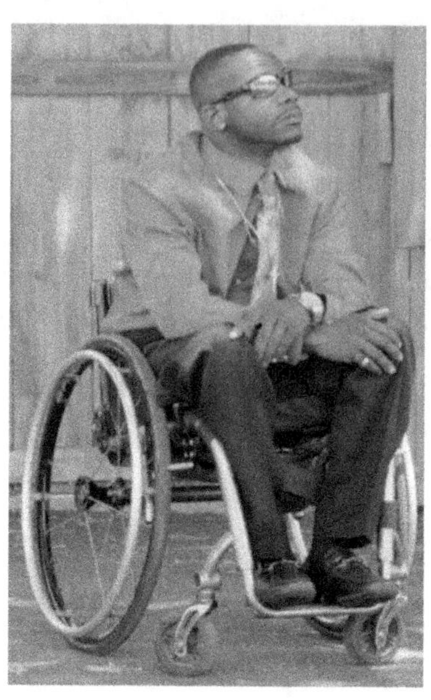

ABOUT THE AUTHOR

I have been writing poetry since I was 12 years old, and I love it. It is a great outlet that I have used to express my thoughts feelings, actions, and emotions. I was born and raised on the Southeast side of Houston, Texas. I was a little bit of a problem child so thus I went to six different elementary schools, but we only moved twice. I attended Hartman Middle School and graduated from Evan E. Worthing High School. I was Poet of the Year in 2002. I have a Bachelor of Science in Business Information Systems.

Please check out my website www.fredleepublishing.com I can be reached at (832) 931-2638 or by email at fredleepublishing@gmail.com